GOOD HOUSEKEEPING
Children's
Cook Book

First published 1958 by Ebury Press
National Magazine House, 72 Broadwick Street, London W1V 2BP
Reprinted 1961
Second edition 1966
Reprinted 1967
Reprinted 1968
Third edition 1969
Fourth edition 1972
Revised edition 1976
Reprinted 1981

ISBN 0 85223 069 9

Photographs by Stephen Baker
Drawings by Ivan Ripley

Acknowledgements to:
Heal's, Guildford
Habitat, Guildford
Design and Craft, Farnham

Printed and bound in Italy by
New Interlitho S.p.a., Milan

GOOD HOUSEKEEPING
Children's Cook Book

by
Rosemary Wadey

with
THE
GOOD HOUSEKEEPING
INSTITUTE

EBURY PRESS
London

Contents

Cooking is Fun

This book is designed to help make cooking easy for you, even if you have never tried cooking before, and make you discover just how much fun it can be.

Everything is explained clearly in pictures as well as in words. If when you first read the recipe through you find some process mentioned that you don't understand, read pages 10 to 23, which tell you how to chop, grate, measure, and so on; how to use the oven and grill in the proper way; how to prepare your baking tins for use; and lots of other things too, which will more than likely answer your questions.

Collect together everything you need before you start, following the list given in each recipe. Getting ready properly is part of the secret of being a good cook—everything gets done in the correct order and the right way.

You must start with clean hands and fingernails, so always remember to wash them thoroughly before you begin to cook. Wear an apron to protect your clothes from getting dirty. It isn't only something you spill which makes a mess, but also jobs like sieving flour or icing sugar and weighing out ingredients.

Don't be disappointed if your cooking doesn't always turn out perfect the first time. You will get better and better at it and very soon may be able to cook a whole meal all by yourself. Remember—if at first you don't succeed, try, try and try again.

One last word, don't forget the washing up. If you want to cook again, leave the kitchen clean and tidy as you found it—then you'll often be welcome.

Have fun!

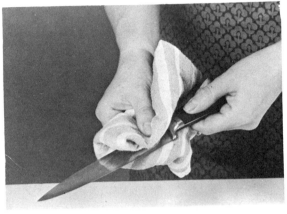

Safety First for Cooks

1 Always wipe a knife from the back of the blade. Never run your fingers along the sharp edge. When carrying a knife, hold it with the blade pointing downwards, in case you should stumble or fall. Always pick up a knife by the handle, never by the blade.

2 To lift up or carry a kettle, put your hand under the handle and grip it firmly, then there can be no risk of being scalded by escaping steam. If the handle is hot, use a cloth to hold it.

3 When putting an electric plug into the socket, make sure the wall switch is turned to OFF and that your hands are completely dry. Then hold the plug as shown in the picture, keeping your fingers well away from the metal pins, and push firmly into the socket. Turn the switch to ON.

4 When saucepans are put on the stove, turn the handles towards the back so that they cannot be knocked off by anyone passing. Always use a thick cloth to lift them off if the handles are hot; use two hands for heavy or very full pans.

How to Use your Cooker

With both **Gas** and **Electric** cookers, the **hob** or top of the cooker usually has three or four **burners** and a **grill.**

Modern **Gas burners** light automatically and so do many grills: you simply push the tap and turn it to light. When the burner is lit, turn it down so that none of the flames show around the edges of the pan; this will save gas and prevent your saucepan burning, but will not slow down the cooking time. Older cookers often have a special gas lighter attached to the side on a cable, which either clicks alight by itself as you take it out of the socket, or lights when you press the trigger.

The **Gas grill** will probably be 'eye-level'. To use it, turn it on full to get really hot first, then turn it down to the temperature required.

The **boiling rings** or **hotplates** on an **Electric cooker** can be solid metal or coiled metal tubes. Make sure the main (wall) switch is on, then switch the hotplate to 'high' to get it really hot before turning it down to the temperature you need. Modern hotplates heat up very quickly, but do not all turn red unless on very high for some time. They are also slow to cool down—so watch your fingers, and don't leave anything on top of the cooker such as a cloth, plastic object or anything which could catch fire, melt or crack.

The **Electric grill** may be 'eye-level' or situated between the top of the cooker and the oven. In many modern cookers it can also be used as a second oven, with separate knobs for use as a grill or an oven. Turn the grill to 'high' and let it get red hot before regulating it for use.

When using the **oven** of either cooker, arrange the shelves so that the tins or casseroles you are using will fit properly and still allow the heat to circulate evenly. For instance, a tray of scones needs only a small space between shelves, but a large casserole or pie will need lots of room.

The **Gas oven burners** are at the back of the oven and are lit in the same way as the rings and grill, depending on whether it is an automatic cooker or not. If it is not automatic, there may be a special hole inside the oven in front at the bottom; turn on the oven gas tap and put the flame of the gas lighter to the hole, which will then light the burners. Make sure the oven tap is turned on full and choose the heat you want by turning the dial to the number stated in your recipe. Allow about 10 minutes for the oven to heat up and then the middle shelf will have reached the correct heat.

With the **Electric oven,** first turn on the main switch and then the oven switch, which shows the temperature markings, and select the temperature stated in the recipe. Most modern cookers have a light which comes on when you turn on the oven and goes out when the oven has reached the correct temperature—it should take 15–20 minutes to heat up.

Always remember to turn off all switches on an **Electric cooker** when you have finished, especially the main switch.

The Right Way to
Use a Knife

Always hold the knife blade downwards.
Always cut away from you, never towards yourself.
Use a proper cutting board or work surface—not formica tops.
Always wipe a knife from the back of the blade.

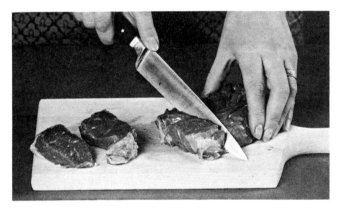

To slice meat, fruit or vegetables, hold the food firmly on a board or table and, with a long-bladed knife, cut in long strokes, keeping the other hand well away from the blade.

This is a different kind of a knife with a flexible blade and no sharp edges. It's called a palette knife and is used for turning pancakes and omelettes in the pan, spreading, and for many other jobs. Different sized palette knives are used for different jobs.

To chop vegetables, nuts, dried fruits, parsley and mint, etc., hold a broad-bladed knife (called a cook's knife or kitchen knife) firmly at the tip of the blade and cut by moving the knife up and down from the handle end. Work on a special chopping board.

To cut fruit or a vegetable into thin slices, hold it firmly on the board and cut downwards with a sharp cook's knife of the appropriate size. Hold the food well behind the blade to keep fingers out of the way and make sure your hands are dry, for wet hands can sometimes slip.

To cut bread into neat slices, use this sharp knife with a serrated edge (called a bread saw or bread knife). Hold the loaf firmly on a board and cut with a sawing movement.

To scrape root vegetables, such as carrots, use a small vegetable knife. Scrape downwards and away from yourself, holding the vegetable firmly in one hand and turning it as required. You should work on a wooden board. New potatoes are held in the left hand and scraped carefully towards you with a small (but not too sharp) vegetable knife held in the right hand.

To Cook...
and all the other Verbs

To baste
Pour hot, melted fat or dripping from a spoon over meat and poultry in a baking tin to keep it moist during roasting.

To beat
Make a sharp stroking movement with a wooden spoon to remove lumps and turn ingredient(s) into a froth, a paste or a batter —depending on what they are. See also *To cream*, page 15.

To bind
Press moistened flour or other ingredients into a sticky ball, using a palette knife and sometimes your fingers.

To blend
Mix dry and wet ingredients together
smoothly with a wooden spoon.

To chop
Cut into small pieces—see page 13.

To combine
Mix together dry ingredients for a cake,
using a palette knife or spoon.

To cream
Mix butter or margarine with another
ingredient, such as sugar, until it becomes
soft, light and creamy.

To dice
Cut into small cubes.

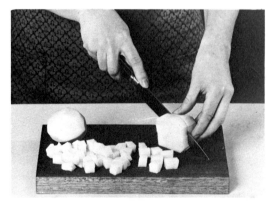

To fold in
Mix things like dried fruit into a cake mixture, or caster sugar into stiffly beaten egg whites.

To glaze
Brush pastry with beaten egg or milk before baking—it makes the cooked pastry golden and shiny.

To grate
Remove peel of a lemon or orange in fine little flakes. For cheese, use a coarser side of the grater; for vegetables for salads, use the coarsest part of all.

To knead
Push and mould sticky lumps of dough between your fingers to get them smooth before rolling.

To peel
Use a sharp vegetable knife—and watch your fingers!

To pipe
Use a piping bag (either buy one or make one from greaseproof paper—see Rabbit Mousses, page 68) with a piping nozzle of the right size and shape placed in the end of the bag. There are many nozzles to choose from, all of which make different patterns. Half-fill the bag with icing, fold up to enclose the icing and squeeze the bag to press icing out through the nozzle to make stars, whirls, shells, etc, for decoration.

To rub in
In pastry-making and with some cakes, literally rub small pieces of fat in flour between your fingers until it turns into fine little lumps which look like breadcrumbs.

To shred
Slice cabbage or other vegetables into thin slices or strands.

To sieve
Use a wooden spoon to push ingredients (ie, soup) through a fine wire mesh strainer —it smoothes out all the lumps. Flour is just shaken through the sieve.

To whip
Beat eggs or cream with a hand-whisk or fork with a light, firm, circular stroke. This is the way you make egg yolks and their whites blend together evenly.

To whisk
Faster way of beating a batter, or whipping cream or egg whites until frothy. This is a rotary whisk, but you can also use an electric hand mixer.

To weigh

Measuring dry ingredients. We tell you how much in metric weights and in pounds and ounces in these recipes. See also page 21.

To measure liquid

Use a jug with the measurements on the side. We tell you how much liquid in litres and pints.

To measure a level spoonful

Use a knife or palette knife to smooth off the surface for an accurate measurement.

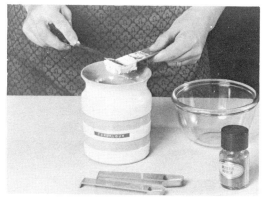

To measure syrup or honey

Warm the spoon, then brush lightly all over with oil. The measured syrup will then slowly slide off the spoon without sticking and altering the measurement.

Basic Equipment

When you decide to do some cooking, you start by reading through the recipe carefully. A quick look will tell you if you have all the ingredients mentioned. Fine. Now look at the list of utensils. You may find that not all the exact items are available, so you will have to find something else which will do the same job and is very similar. All kitchens have basic equipment like kitchen scales and a measuring jug, which you must have for accurate weighing and measuring to make the recipes work—it's no use just guessing, for that would only be a disaster and waste of ingredients!

Mixing bowls and basins can be of any size, although the ones used in the pictures in the book are the best size for the particular job if they are available. But don't worry if you have to use a different size—it won't affect the result of your cooking.

Knives are very important, for you can't cut up or chop anything without them; but again, if you haven't the ones suggested on pages 12 to 13 or in the pictures, find something else suitable and similar.

A chopping board of some sort is essential for any cutting up or chopping, to protect the working surface from cuts and scratches. They can be of wood or some type of laminated board, often with attractive decorations.

A palette knife or fish slice is necessary for removing biscuits from a baking sheet or fish fingers from a pan, as well as for loosening a cake from a tin or levelling the top of something before putting it in the oven. But if you haven't one, use a round-bladed table knife. Remember that oven gloves or a thick cloth are most essential when touching anything hot, or badly burnt fingers would result.

A wire rack is necessary for cooling cooked cakes, biscuits, etc. If they are left to cool in the tin, all the steam and heat is absorbed back into the food, causing it to go soggy. A wire rack enables air to circulate the food and so prevents this. As soon as it is completely cold it should be stored in an airtight container.

Do not stand hot things straight from the oven or a boiling saucepan on a formica or other surface which may be damaged by the excess heat. Always find a pot rest or chopping board to stand it on and thus prevent any damage.

Metric Equivalents

This book has been written for you with the ingredients shown first in metric weights and then in imperial measurements, which are enclosed in the brackets. Before you start, decide which type of measurement you are going to use and then keep to it throughout the recipe. Your mother's kitchen scales may only have pounds and ounces marked, in which case follow all the weights and measurements given in the brackets.

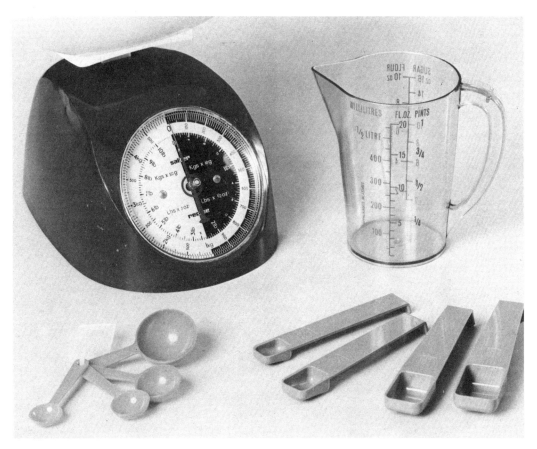

Kitchen scales, measuring jug, imperial measuring spoons,
and *bottom right* metric measuring spoons

Preparing Tins for Baking

To grease a baking sheet
Rub the surface with a piece of butter or margarine paper with a little fat still left on it, *or* brush all over with melted lard or white fat or with oil, using a pastry brush. Baking sheets with a special non-stick surface do not need greasing.

To dredge with flour
Grease as above, then tip a little flour into the centre of the tin. Knock the edges against your hand until the whole surface is covered with flour. Turn tin over and knock out any excess flour.

To grease patty tins
Brush inside each patty tin with oil or melted fat, paying particular attention to the corners where the cake is likely to stick. If you use paper cake cases inside the patty tins, no greasing is necessary.

To line cake tins
Place tin on double greaseproof paper and draw around the base. Cut out these circles with kitchen scissors. Brush inside of tins with oil or melted fat. Place paper circle carefully in the base and brush with oil. This prevents the bottom of the cake sticking to the tin. Peel paper off when cake is removed from the tin.

Here's How to Start

First decide what you want to make. Next, read through the recipe and see
if you have all the ingredients. Now see if you need to use the oven; if you
do, light it or switch it on, then turn it to the temperature stated in the
recipe so that it can heat up while you're preparing everything.
Read the recipe through again and collect together all the utensils you
will need (they are written beside the ingredients in each recipe). If the list
mentions something you can't find in the kitchen, use something as near to it
as possible. If you can't find a square cake tin, use a round one a size larger.
If you can't find a whisk, use a fork—it may take a bit longer but will still
enable you to make the recipe. No round cutters? Use the top of a tumbler
or mug which is nearest the size you need. It doesn't matter if you have to
use substitute utensils as long as they are similar in size or shape or do the
same thing: the pots and pans aren't the most important part of cookery.
Now collect together all the ingredients and weigh out the amounts
stated in the recipe. You are now ready to start—follow the step by step
pictures and your cooking is under way. Remember, as soon as you have
finished cooking clear everything away, do all the washing and drying up
and pack it all away tidily. Leave the kitchen neat and tidy and then you'll
be allowed to cook again another day.

Gingerbread Men

Ingredients
300 g (12 oz) plain flour
1 level teaspoonful bicarbonate of soda
2 level teaspoonfuls ground ginger
100 g (4 oz) butter or margarine
150 g (6 oz) soft brown sugar
4 tablespoonfuls golden syrup
1 egg
currants

Utensils
2 baking sheets
gingerbread man cutter or
   greaseproof paper and scissors
teaspoon
sieve
mixing bowl
knife
tablespoon

basin
small saucepan
fork
flour dredger
rolling pin
small kitchen knife
palette knife
wire rack

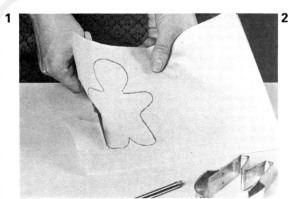

1 Grease baking sheets. If you haven't a gingerbread man cutter, cut a shape from greaseproof paper for a pattern.

2 Mix flour, soda and ginger, sieve into bowl. Cut in fat and rub into dry ingredients till mixture looks like breadcrumbs.

3 Mix in sugar. Warm syrup in a basin over hot water, beat in the egg. Add to bowl, mixing to a pliable dough.

4 Knead lightly on floured surface, roll out to 0·5 cm ($\frac{1}{4}$ in) thick. Cut round paper shape with knife (or use cutter).

5 Lift men on to baking sheets with palette knife, keeping well apart. Mark eyes, mouth and buttons with currants.

6 Bake at 190°C (375°F) mark 5 for 10–15 minutes till pale golden brown. Cool slightly then carefully move to wire rack.

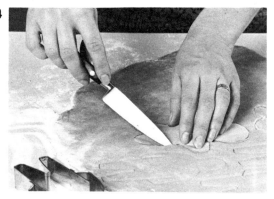

Coconut Pyramids

Ingredients
2 eggs, separated (see picture 1)
100 g (4 oz) caster sugar
150 g (6 oz) desiccated coconut
rice paper
pink colouring

Utensils
large mixing bowl
small basin
rotary whisk or electric hand mixer
tablespoon
1 large or 2 small baking sheets
skewer
palette knife

1 Crack one of the eggs on the side of the large bowl and let just the white drop into the bowl through the half-open shell.

2 Keep the yolk in the half shell until the egg has separated, then put the yolk in a small basin. Repeat with second egg.

3 Whisk the whites until they are thick and form "peaks". Spoon in the sugar and whisk again very thoroughly.

4 Mix in coconut with spoon. Line baking sheets with rice paper. Put 8 spoonfuls of mixture on to sheet, forming pyramids.

5 Tint the other half of mixture with a little colouring, using tip of skewer; place in pyramids on baking sheet as before.

6 Bake in the oven at 150°C (300°F) mark 2 for 1 hour until pale brown, then cool. Trim off surplus rice paper before serving.

Shortbread

Ingredients

150 g (6 oz) plain flour
pinch of salt
100 g (4 oz) butter
50 g (2 oz) caster sugar
fine sugar to dust top of
shortbread

Utensils

sieve
mixing bowl
knife
baking sheet
flour dredger
rolling pin

fork
kitchen knife
palette knife
wire rack
shortbread mould (if you have one)

*Pictures 5 and 6 show you an alternative way
to shape the mixture using a shortbread
mould — if you have one.*

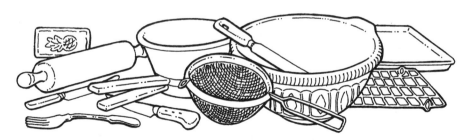

1 Sieve flour and salt into the mixing bowl. Cut butter into pieces and rub in until the mixture looks like breadcrumbs.

2 Mix in sugar. Knead mixture till it forms a ball and becomes smooth and pliable. Grease and flour the baking sheet.

3 On a floured surface, roll out the mixture to about 1 cm ($\frac{1}{2}$ in) thick. Place on baking sheet, crimp (pinch up) edge with fingers.

4 Prick it all over with fork. Bake in the oven at 150°C (300°F) mark 2 for 1 hour. When cooked, cut into 8 pieces, cool on rack.

5 If you use a wooden mould, flour it well. Put in the mixture, pressing it well into the scalloped edging.

6 Slice off any surplus dough; turn on to sheet. Bake as above but for only $\frac{3}{4}$ hour. Dredge all shortbread with fine sugar.

Cheese Straws

Ingredients
150 g (6 oz) plain flour
$\frac{1}{4}$ level teaspoonful salt
good pinch of cayenne pepper
50 g (2 oz) Cheddar cheese
75 g (3 oz) margarine
about 3 tablespoonfuls water

Utensils
sieve
mixing bowl
teaspoon
baking sheet
grater
knife

tablespoon
palette knife
flour dredger
rolling pin
kitchen knife
wire rack

*Small circles approx 2·5–4 cm (1–1$\frac{1}{2}$ in)
can also be cut from the cheese pastry to
make biscuits. Cook for about 15 minutes.*

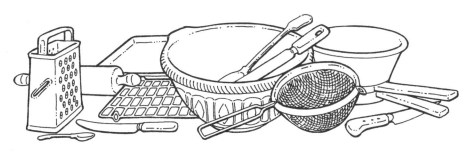

1 Sieve flour, salt and pepper into mixing bowl. Lightly grease the baking sheet. Grate the cheese finely.

2 Cut the margarine into pieces, add to the flour and rub in till mixture looks like fine breadcrumbs.

3 Add the cheese and mix thoroughly. Add sufficient water to mix to a pliable dough, using palette knife.

4 Knead lightly, on a floured surface, roll out to about 0·5 cm ($\frac{1}{4}$ in) thick. Cut into strips 12·5 cm (5 in) by 1 cm ($\frac{1}{2}$ in).

5 Carefully twist each strip of pastry twice and place on the baking sheet.

6 Bake at 200°C (400°F) mark 6 for about 15 minutes till golden brown. Remove carefully to wire rack.

1

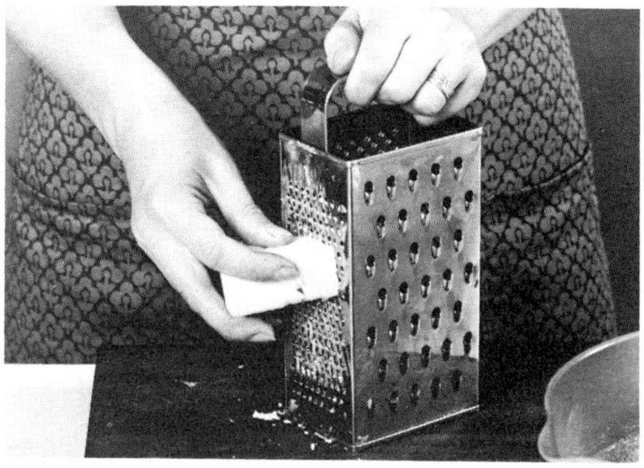

2

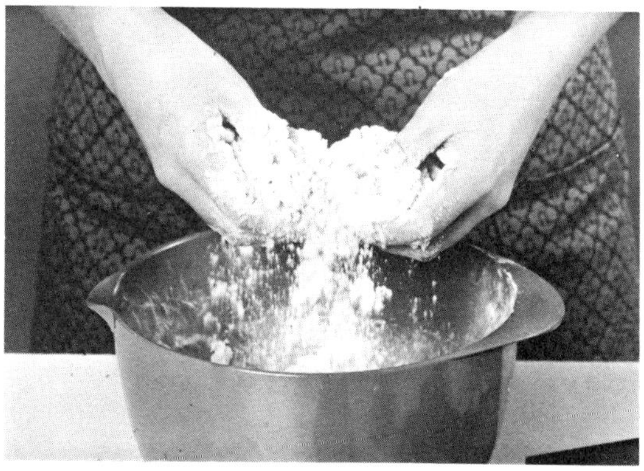

3

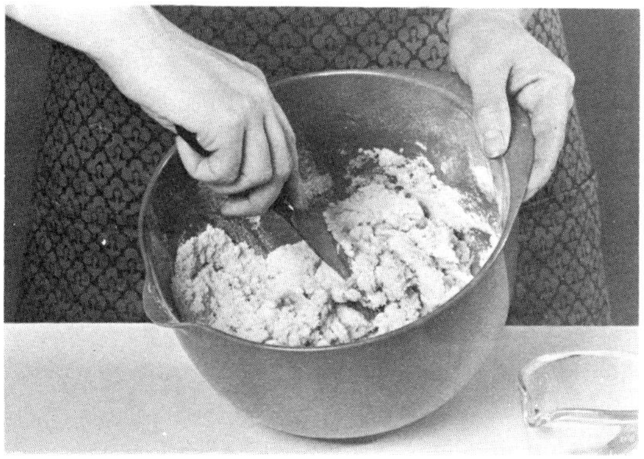

4

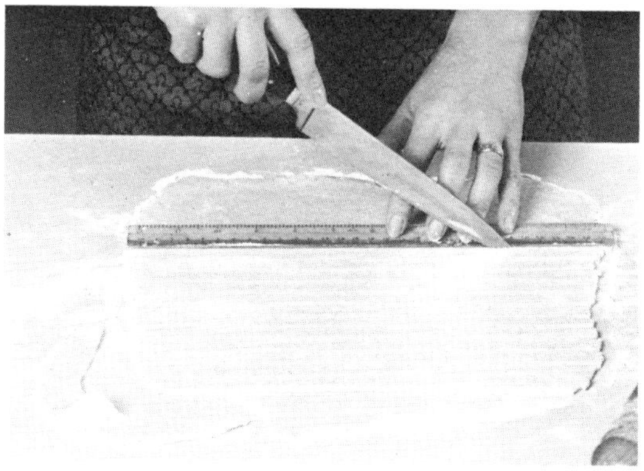

5

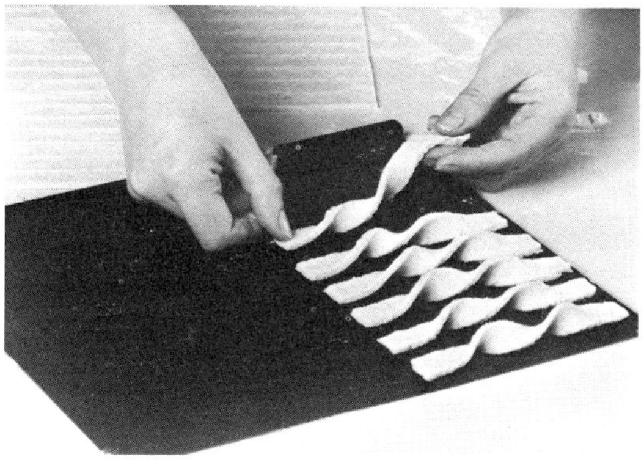

6

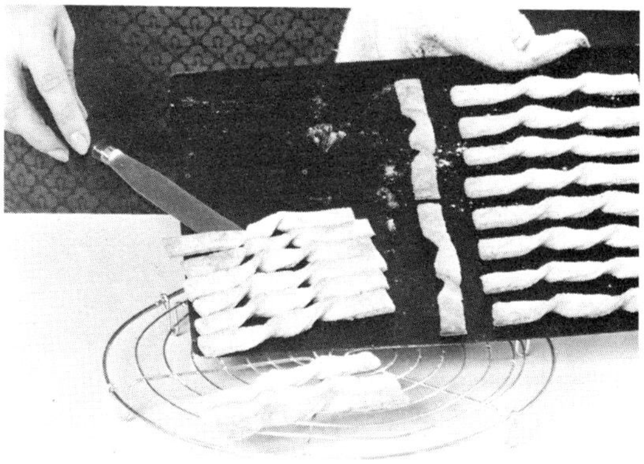

Flapjacks

Ingredients

100 g (4 oz) margarine
25 g (1 oz) caster sugar
2 tablespoonfuls golden syrup
200 g (8 oz) rolled oats
pinch of salt

Utensils

mixing bowl
wooden spoon
baking tin, shallow
   20 cm (8 in) square
tablespoon

basin
saucepan
palette knife
kitchen knife

*To warm a basin over hot water—see 2—
it's safest first to heat a little water in the
saucepan then turn off the heat just before
the water boils. Rest the basin in or on top of
the saucepan.*

1 Cream together the margarine and sugar until the mixture is very soft. Grease the baking tin.

2 Put the syrup in a basin and warm over a pan of hot water until it becomes runny. Add it to the creamed mixture.

3 Now gradually work in the rolled oats and the salt until they have all been used. Mix thoroughly.

4 Put the mixture into the baking tin, pressing it down very carefully into the corners.

5 Smooth the surface with a palette knife and bake in the oven at 190°C (375°F) mark 5 for 30–40 minutes.

6 Take from the oven when firm and golden brown and cut into fingers, but leave in the tin until quite cold before removing.

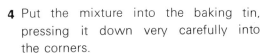

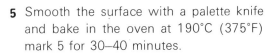

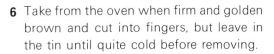

Bumblies

Ingredients
50 g (2 oz) butter
25 g (1 oz) caster sugar
75 g (3 oz) plain flour, sieved
currants
chocolate buttons

Pastry can be rolled out on to a formica or other smooth surface or a pastry board it preferred.

Utensils
mixing bowl
wooden spoon
palette knife
flour dredger
rolling pin
baking sheet
6-cm (2½-in) diameter plain cutter
vegetable knife
wire rack

1 Cream butter thoroughly with wooden spoon. Add sugar and beat together till fluffy. Add half the flour, mix well.

2 Add remaining flour and mix to a dough, binding together with palette knife. Knead till smooth on floured surface.

3 Carefully roll out dough to about 0·25 cm ($\frac{1}{8}$ in) thick—lightly flouring rolling pin to prevent sticking, and cut into rounds.

4 Using palette knife transfer to lightly greased baking sheet. Mark features with cutter. Use currants for eyes and nose.

5 Cut arm shapes. Gently pull away from sides. Bake in the oven at 170°C (325°F) mark 3 for 20 minutes. Cool on wire rack.

6 Fix feet by using a warmed knife to make a slit across the chocolate buttons. Hold each Bumblie in slit until set.

Peanut Butter Cookies

Ingredients

50 g (2 oz) smooth peanut butter
50 g (2 oz) butter
50 g (2 oz) caster sugar
40 g (1½ oz) light soft brown sugar
1 small orange
1 large egg (but use only HALF the egg)
40 g (1½ oz) raisins
100 g (4 oz) self raising flour

Utensils

mixing bowl
grater
wooden spoon
small basin
fork
chopping board
kitchen knife
sieve

2 baking sheets
palette knife
wire rack

1 Place peanut butter, butter and both sugars in mixing bowl. Finely grate the rind from orange and add to bowl.

2 Cream mixture until light and fluffy. Beat the egg in a basin with a fork. Beat only HALF the egg into mixture.

3 Chop raisins then add to mixture. Sieve flour into bowl and mix everything together to make a fairly firm dough.

4 Roll dough in your hands into small balls about the size of a walnut. Place well apart on ungreased baking sheets.

5 Dip a fork in a little flour and press crisscross lines on to each biscuit, flattening them.

6 Bake at 180°C (350°F) mark 4 for 25 minutes till risen and golden. Remove with a palette knife and cool on wire rack.

Boston Brownies

Ingredients
50 g (2 oz) plain chocolate, broken into pieces
65 g (2½ oz) butter or margarine
150 g (6 oz) caster sugar
65 g (2½ oz) self raising flour
¼ level teaspoonful salt
2 eggs
½ teaspoonful vanilla essence
50 g (2 oz) shelled walnuts

Utensils
20-cm (8-in) shallow square tin
flour dredger
2 basins
small saucepan
wooden spoon
teaspoon
sieve
mixing bowl
fork
chopping board
kitchen knife
palette knife

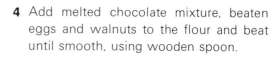

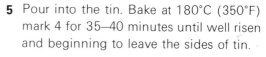

1 Grease tin and lightly dredge with flour. Put chocolate in basin with butter and melt over pan of hot water. Beat in sugar.

2 Mix flour and salt and sieve into bowl. Beat eggs in a basin with fork. Add vanilla essence.

3 Roughly chop up the walnuts on the wooden chopping board, using the kitchen knife.

4 Add melted chocolate mixture, beaten eggs and walnuts to the flour and beat until smooth, using wooden spoon.

5 Pour into the tin. Bake at 180°C (350°F) mark 4 for 35—40 minutes until well risen and beginning to leave the sides of tin.

6 Cool in the tin. Carefully cut into 12 fingers when cold and remove from tin using the palette knife.

Truffles

Ingredients
100 g (4 oz) stale cake or any cake
  crumbs
1 small orange
25 g (1 oz) glacé cherries
50 g (2 oz) caster sugar
25 g (1 oz) ground almonds
4 level tablespoonfuls apricot jam
1 teaspoonful water
chocolate vermicelli (plain and milk
  varieties)

Utensils
grater
mixing bowl
chopping board
kitchen knife
palette knife
tablespoon
teaspoon
small saucepan
sieve
wooden spoon

baking sheet
waxed paper
small polythene bag or small bowl
paper sweet cases

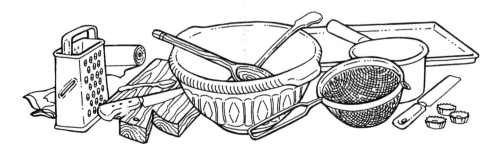

1 Rub cake or crumbs through fine side of grater. Grate orange finely. Put crumbs and orange rind into bowl.

2 Finely chop the cherries. Add to the crumbs with sugar and almonds and mix well.

3 Melt apricot jam and water in a small saucepan until runny. Sieve this jam into the cake crumbs.

4 Mix the jam and crumbs until evenly blended and then bind together with the palette knife.

5 Shape mixture into small even-sized balls, in the hands, and stand on a baking sheet covered with waxed paper.

6 Dip truffles into vermicelli until completely coated. Replace on waxed paper and leave to dry. Serve in paper cases.

Coconut Ice

Ingredients
400 g (1 lb) granulated sugar
125 ml ($\frac{1}{4}$ pt) water
100 g (4 oz) desiccated coconut
butter for greasing the tin
pink colouring

Utensils
measuring jug
saucepan
wooden spoon
glass
small deep loaf tin about 15 cm by 9 cm
   (6 in by $3\frac{1}{2}$ in)
palette knife
skewer
kitchen knife

1 Put the sugar and water in the saucepan and heat slowly until the sugar has dissolved. Bring to boil for 3 minutes.

2 Test a drop of the syrup in a glass of cold water. It should form a soft ball. If it doesn't, boil for ½ minute and re-test.

3 Take off the heat and mix in the coconut. Stir while the mixture cools and whitens. Grease the loaf tin with butter.

4 When the mixture is really thick, quickly put half of it into the greased tin and level off the top with a palette knife.

5 Colour remaining mixture pink, using a skewer, and very quickly spread it on top of the white coconut ice. Press well down.

6 Put the tin in a cool place and leave to set. When it is cold, cut the coconut ice into fingers and then remove from the tin.

Chocolate Fudge

Ingredients
400 g (1 lb) granulated sugar
125 g (5 oz) butter
125 ml ($\frac{1}{4}$ pt) milk
100 g (4 oz) plain chocolate, broken
   into pieces
2 tablespoonfuls thin honey

Utensils
measuring jug
tablespoon
large heavy saucepan
wooden spoon
shallow baking tin 20 cm (8 in) square
cup
kitchen knife
paper sweet cases

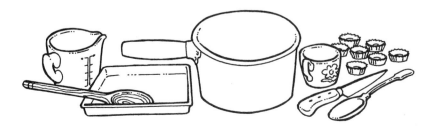

1 Put sugar, butter, milk, chocolate and honey in saucepan and heat gently till sugar has dissolved. Grease the tin.

2 Bring mixture to the boil, stirring constantly. Boil fast for 15 minutes, but don't let the fudge boil over.

3 Test some in a cup of cold water to see if it forms a soft ball. If not, continue boiling until it does.

4 Remove pan from heat and stand on a cool surface for 5 minutes (protect formica surfaces). Beat hard with wooden spoon.

5 Keep beating until mixture thickens and feels rough. Scrape it to the edge of the saucepan and pour into the tin.

6 Leave in a cool place to set. Mark into squares, cut into pieces and put in paper cases. Store in an airtight container.

Toffees and Toffee Apples

Ingredients
50 g (2 oz) butter
400 g (1 lb) brown sugar
2 teaspoonfuls vinegar
125 ml ($\frac{1}{4}$ pt) water
1 tablespoonful golden syrup
6 apples

Utensils
20-cm (8-in) shallow square tin
teaspoon
measuring jug
tablespoon
large strong saucepan
wooden spoon
kitchen knife

chopping board
old knife
hammer or weight
waxed or cellophane paper
wooden sticks

If you are unable to get hold of wooden toffee apple sticks, use "dowel" (·45 cm/$\frac{3}{16}$in thick) available from do-it-yourself shops and cut it into 12·5–15 cm (5–6 in) lengths. After use, wash thoroughly and keep until required again.

1. Butter the tin. Put all ingredients except apples in saucepan. Heat slowly till dissolved. Bring to boil, stirring.

2. Boil for 5 minutes. Test few drops of syrup in jug of cold water to see if it forms hard ball when pressed between fingers.

3. If necessary, continue boiling the syrup for a few minutes to reach this "hard ball" stage, then pour into greased tin.

4. After 5 minutes, or when toffee begins to harden, mark into squares with greased knife. Leave till set and hard.

5. Remove toffee from tin. Using very old knife and hammer or weight, break it up and wrap in waxed or cellophane paper.

6. For toffee apples, push sticks into cores and twirl in hot toffee. Cool on waxed paper. Wrap in cellophane when hard.

Soda Bread

Ingredients

400 g (1 lb) plain flour
2 level teaspoonfuls bicarbonate of soda
2 level teaspoonfuls cream of tartar
1 level teaspoonful salt
50 g (2 oz) lard
300 ml ($\frac{1}{2}$ pt) milk
1 tablespoonful lemon juice

Utensils

teaspoon	lemon squeezer
sieve	palette knife
wooden spoon	flour dredger
mixing bowl	baking sheet
knife	kitchen knife
measuring jug	wire rack

*To make brown soda bread use 200 g
(8 oz) plain flour and 200 g (8 oz)
wholemeal flour and proceed as for white
soda bread.*

1 Mix together flour, bicarbonate of soda, cream of tartar and salt and sieve them into a mixing bowl.

2 Cut lard into small pieces and rub into the flour until the mixture looks like fine breadcrumbs.

3 Add lemon juice to milk (to make it go sour). Add to bowl and mix to soft but manageable dough with palette knife.

4 Turn on to a floured surface and with the hands shape into a circle about 17·5 cm (7 in) across.

5 Grease the baking sheet and place dough carefully on it. Mark into quarters with a sharp knife.

6 Bake at 220°C (425°F) mark 7 for about 30 minutes till risen and golden. Cool on wire rack. Eat while fresh.

Scones

Ingredients

200 g (8 oz) flour, plain or self raising
$\frac{1}{4}$ level teaspoonful salt
3 level teaspoonfuls baking powder
  (leave this out if you're using self
  raising flour)
25 g (1 oz) butter
125 ml ($\frac{1}{4}$ pt) milk
milk to glaze

Utensils

teaspoon
sieve
bowl
wooden spoon
knife
baking sheet
measuring jug
palette knife
flour dredger
5-cm (2-in) diameter
  plain cutter
basin
fork
pastry brush
wire rack

VARIATIONS
Cheese – *add 40 g (1$\frac{1}{2}$ oz) finely*
grated Cheddar cheese at the end of
Stage 2, then continue as above.
Fruit – add 50 g (2 oz) sultanas or
currants at the end of Stage 2, then
continue as above.

1 Mix flour and salt (and baking powder, if you're using plain flour) and sieve into a bowl. Cut butter into pieces.

2 Using fingers, rub the butter into the dry mixture till it looks like breadcrumbs. Grease the baking sheet.

3 Make a well in the mixture and gradually add the milk, mixing with a palette knife to form a soft dough.

4 Turn out on to a floured surface and knead lightly. Form it into a flat round about 2 cm ($\frac{3}{4}$ in) thick.

5 Using the cutter, cut the dough into small rounds and place them on the baking sheet.

6 Brush the scones with milk. Bake in the oven at 220°C (425°F) mark 7 for 8–10 minutes. Cool on wire rack.

Rock Buns

Ingredients

200 g (8 oz) flour, plain or self raising
2 level teaspoonfuls baking powder
(leave this out if you're using self
raising flour)
pinch of salt
pinch of mixed spice
pinch of nutmeg
50 g (2 oz) currants
100 g (4 oz) margarine
75 g (3 oz) sugar
25 g (1 oz) chopped mixed peel
1 egg
little milk if necessary

Utensils

teaspoon
sieve
mixing bowl
grater (if you're using whole nutmeg)
knife
fork
basin
baking sheet
wire rack

*Bought ready-washed currants do not need
cleaning (stage 2).*

1 If you're using plain flour, measure baking powder into it. Add salt to flour and sieve into bowl, with mixed spice and nutmeg.

2 Clean currants by putting them in sieve with extra flour. Rub well, then shake off surplus flour into any container.

3 Cut margarine into pieces and rub into the flour until it looks like fine bread-crumbs.

4 Add sugar, currants and peel, mixing them well. Beat the egg with a fork in a basin.

5 Add to dry ingredients, mix well. Mixture should be fairly firm and dry—add milk if necessary. Grease baking sheet.

6 Put mixture in small heaps on the baking sheet and bake for 15–20 minutes at 200°C (400°F) mark 6. Cool on wire rack.

Chocolate Butterfly Cakes

Ingredients

100 g (4 oz) margarine
100 g (4 oz) caster sugar
2 eggs
100 g (4 oz) flour, plain or self raising
½ level teaspoonful baking powder (leave this out if you're using self raising flour)

25 g (1 oz) cocoa
1 tablespoonful water
50 g (2 oz) butter
100 g (4 oz) sieved icing sugar
vanilla essence

Utensils

patty tins
mixing bowl
wooden spoon
small basin
teaspoon
sieve
tablespoon
wire rack
kitchen knife
palette knife

To make the plain butterfly cakes shown on the cover make a Victoria Sandwich mixture (see page 58), put the mixture into patty tins (with or without paper cases) and cook as opposite. To assemble, use half the lemon butter icing (see the note on Victoria Sandwich, page 58) or coffee or chocolate butter icing. Decorate with chocolate buttons and angelica and a dusting of icing sugar, if you prefer.

1 Grease patty tins. Cream together margarine and caster sugar. Add eggs one at a time. Beat thoroughly.

2 Measure baking powder (if used) and add to flour and cocoa. Sieve all these to make sure they are well mixed.

3 Fold dry ingredients into creamed mixture. Add water and blend well until it forms a soft, dropping consistency.

4 Divide mixture between tins. Bake in the oven at 190°C (375°F) mark 5 for 15—20 minutes till firm. Turn out and cool.

5 To make icing, cream butter with icing sugar; add 3 drops vanilla. Slice off top of each cake and cut slice down middle.

6 Spread icing on each cake with palette knife. Place "butterfly wings" on top, with their curved sides together.

Nutty Fruit Meringues

Ingredients
50 g (2 oz) whole almonds
25 g (1 oz) glacé cherries
butter and flour for baking sheet
110 g (4½ oz) icing sugar
2 egg whites (see how to separate
eggs on page 27)

Utensils
saucepan
chopping board
kitchen knife
baking sheet
sieve
mixing bowl
rotary or spiral whisk
   or electric hand
   mixer

tablespoon
teaspoon
wire rack

*To save time, you can use almonds which
are sold ready-chopped or flaked.
These meringues can be topped with a
whirl or spoonful of whipped cream and a
whole strawberry for special occasions.*

1 Put the almonds in boiling water and let them stand for 2 minutes. Drain off hot water and dip them in cold water.

2 The skins will easily peel off (all this is called "blanching" almonds). Chop them into small pieces and put to one side.

3 Cut cherries into quarters. Butter baking sheet and dust lightly with flour. Sift sugar into mixing bowl, add egg whites.

4 Using the rotary or spiral whisk or electric mixer, beat egg whites and icing sugar over hot water till very stiff and dry.

5 Mix cherries with almonds. Using a spoon, fold them into the beaten egg whites until evenly mixed.

6 Shape teaspoonfuls of mixture into mounds on baking sheet. Bake at 170°C (325°F) mark 3 for about 20 minutes.

Victoria Sponge Sandwich

Ingredients

100 g (4 oz) flour, plain or self raising
$\frac{1}{2}$ level teaspoonful baking powder (leave this out if you're using self raising flour)
100 g (4 oz) butter or margarine
100 g (4 oz) caster sugar (plus some for dusting the cake)
2 large eggs
finely grated rind of 1 orange or lemon, optional
jam

Utensils

two 18·5-cm (7-in) sandwich tins
scissors
greaseproof paper
sieve
teaspoon
wooden spoon
mixing bowl
basin
fork
palette knife
wire rack
tablespoon

To make a coffee sponge, add 1 tablespoonful coffee essence to the mixture with the eggs. To make coffee butter icing, soften 50 g (2 oz) butter in a basin, beat in 1 tablespoonful coffee essence and then 125–150 g (5–6 oz) sieved icing sugar. Use to sandwich cakes together and to cover the top.

To make the cake on the cover: use double the mixture and cook in two 20–22$\frac{1}{2}$ cm (8–8$\frac{1}{2}$ in) deep sandwich tins for 25–30 minutes. Leave to cool. Make lemon butter icing by beating together 100 g (4 oz) butter, 225 g (8 oz) sieved icing sugar and a few drops each of lemon essence and yellow colouring. Sandwich the cakes together with lemon curd and half the butter icing. Spread the top with the remaining butter icing and decorate with piped whirls of icing, candles and chocolate buttons.

1 Grease tins, cut greaseproof paper to line bases, grease. Sieve flour and baking powder. Cream fat and sugar till fluffy.

2 Beat eggs in a basin and slowly beat into the creamed mixture. Fold in the flour to give a soft dropping consistency.

3 Fold in orange or lemon rind if you want to give the cake a different flavour. Divide mixture evenly between the tins.

4 Level the tops of the cakes carefully and bake in the oven at 190°C (375°F) mark 5 for 20–25 minutes.

5 Cakes should be firm to the touch, golden brown and well-risen. Turn out carefully and place on a wire rack to cool.

6 When cakes are cold, sandwich together with 2–3 tablespoonfuls of jam. Sprinkle the top lightly with caster sugar.

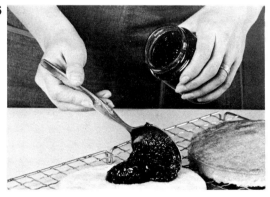

Iced Chocolate Sponge

Ingredients

Sponge

100 g (4 oz) margarine
100 g (4 oz) caster sugar
2 eggs
100 g (4 oz) flour, plain or self raising
½ level teaspoonful baking powder
   (leave this out if you're using self
   raising flour)
25 g (1 oz) cocoa
1 tablespoon water

Icing

100 g (4 oz) plain chocolate, broken
   into pieces
40 g (1½ oz) butter
200 g (8 oz) sieved icing sugar
2 tablespoonfuls warm water
cake decorations—silver balls and
   angelica

Utensils

two 18·5-cm (7-in) sandwich tins
scissors
greaseproof paper
mixing bowl
wooden spoon
3 basins
teaspoon
sieve
tablespoon
wire rack
small saucepan
palette knife
plate
forcing bag with star nozzle

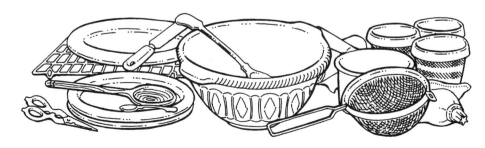

1 Grease and line tins. Make sponge as Chocolate Butterfly Cakes (page 55). Spread in tins, bake as Victoria Sandwich. (page 59).

2 Cool cakes on wire racks. Put chocolate in basin and melt over pan of hot water. Cool. Cream butter and half icing sugar.

3 Beat in half cooled chocolate. Spread most of icing over one cake, sandwich together. Place on wire rack over plate.

4 Add water and sugar to chocolate; mixture should coat back of spoon; add more sugar or water if necessary. Pour on cake.

5 Let icing run smoothly over top. Dip palette knife in hot water and smooth sides only. Fit piping bag with nozzle.

6 Place a few decorations on top of cake. Put rest of icing in bag. Press down and pipe stars on cake top and at base.

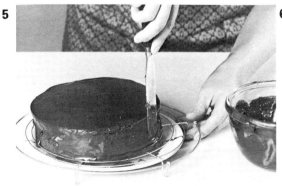

Fruit Jelly

Ingredients
standard packet of jelly
boiling water
can of mandarin oranges
small can of red cherries; 100 g (4 oz)
    fresh cherries; or a small jar of
    maraschino cherries
1 banana
100 g (4 oz) green grapes

Utensils
kitchen scissors   kitchen knife
measuring jug   chopping board
kettle   plate
tablespoon   bowl
jelly mould   serving plate
can opener

The mould can be brushed very lightly with oil instead of rinsing out with cold water, if you prefer.

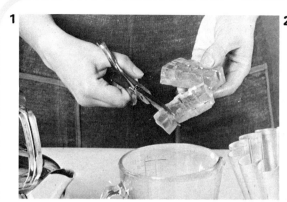

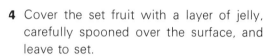

1. Break or cut up jelly and place in jug. Use boiling water to make as directed on packet, stirring well until dissolved.

2. Rinse out mould with cold water then pour in a little jelly. Leave to set. Drain oranges, stone cherries and slice banana.

3. Cut grapes in half and remove pips. Put a little jelly on a plate, dip some fruit in it, then arrange in mould. Leave to set.

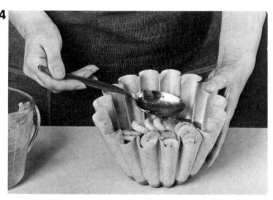

4. Cover the set fruit with a layer of jelly, carefully spooned over the surface, and leave to set.

5. Repeat process till all fruit and jelly are used. Leave to set. It will turn out better if chilled for 6 hours after setting.

6. Loosen edges with fingers then immerse mould in hot water while counting to 5. Put upside-down on plate and shake out.

Chocolate Blancmange

Ingredients
25 g (1 oz) cocoa
40 g (1½ oz) sugar, caster or granulated
40 g (1½ oz) cornflour
568 ml (1 pt) milk
whipped double cream

Utensils
sieve
basin
wooden spoon
saucepan
mould or basin
serving plate

1 Sieve cocoa and place in basin with sugar, cornflour and a little of the milk. Mix until completely smooth.

2 Put rest of milk in saucepan and bring *just* to boil. Pour on to cocoa mixture, stirring well. Return all to saucepan.

3 Bring back to boil, stirring all the time as it thickens, or it will stick and burn. Boil for 2 minutes. Remove from heat.

4 Rinse out mould with cold water, pour in blancmange. Leave in cool place to set for at least 2 hours; it can be left overnight.

5 When blancmange has set firmly, loosen gently around edge—tilt mould sideways, gently touching top with fingers.

6 Turn out on to a serving plate and keep in a cool place until needed. Decorate with whirls of stiffly whipped cream.

Chocolate Pots

Ingredients
125 g (5 oz) plain chocolate
2 large eggs
2 teaspoonfuls coffee essence
150 ml ($\frac{1}{4}$ pt) double cream

Utensils
2 basins
small saucepan
wooden spoon
1 small basin
rotary whisk or electric hand mixer
tablespoon
4 small serving dishes
grater
piping bag and large star nozzle

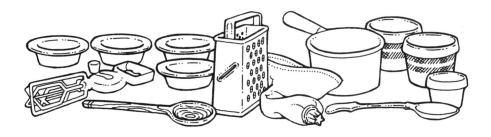

1 Break up 100 g (4 oz) chocolate and put in basin. Place over a saucepan of hot water until melted. Beat until smooth.

2 Separate the eggs (see page 27), putting the whites in a large basin and the yolks in a small basin.

3 Beat coffee essence into melted chocolate until quite smooth then beat in egg yolks, followed by 4 tablespoonfuls of cream.

4 Whisk the egg whites until stiff and firm. Fold carefully and evenly through the chocolate mixture.

5 Pour the chocolate mixture into 4 small serving dishes and chill until set. Grate remaining chocolate.

6 Whip remaining cream until stiff. Fill piping bag, pipe whirls on chocolate pots and sprinkle with grated chocolate.

Rabbit Mousses

Ingredients

1 standard packet of jelly (any flavour)
boiling water
50 g (2 oz) chocolate dots or plain
    chocolate
12 marshmallows
1 family block of frozen mousse or dairy
    ice cream (any flavour)
6 plain chocolate finger biscuits

Utensils

measuring jug
kettle
2 tablespoons
dish for setting jelly
basin
saucepan

greaseproof paper
    piping bag (see note)
kitchen scissors
chopping board
6 small serving plates
knife

*To make your greaseproof paper bag, cut a
piece of paper 25 cm (10 in) square and fold
into a triangle. Roll it into a shape like an ice
cream cone; fold down the points at the top
so they hold it in shape and fix outside edge
with sticky tape.*

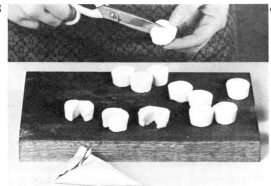

1 Make up jelly as directed on packet, using boiling water. Stir till dissolved, pour into dish and leave to set.

2 Put chocolate dots or broken up chocolate in basin over saucepan of hot water till melted. Place in greaseproof bag.

3 Dip scissors in hot water and cut 6 of the marshmallows almost (but not quite) in half. These are used for the ''ears''.

4 Cut just the tip off the piping bag and carefully pipe rabbit faces on to uncut marshmallows. Leave till chocolate sets.

5 Unwrap mousse or ice cream, cut into 6 and put on plates. Top with a face and ears. Halve biscuits and arrange as legs.

6 Chop jelly with knife. Spoon it around mousses or ice cream. Eat mousses when soft; eat ice cream at once.

Strawberry and Orange Cups

Ingredients
2 medium sized oranges
½ standard packet orange jelly
100 g (4 oz) cake crumbs
200 g (8 oz) strawberries
125-ml (¼-pt) carton double cream
8 small chocolate-orange or chocolate-
   peppermint sticks

Utensils
knife
chopping board
lemon squeezer
measuring jug
kettle
spoons
tablespoon
tablespoon measure
3 basins
rotary whisk
piping bag and 1-cm (½-in)
   star nozzle
4 serving dishes

*To make cake crumbs, either grate stale plain cake on the
medium side of the grater; put in an electric liquidizer
until reduced to crumbs; or rub through a coarse sieve or
colander.*

1 Cut oranges in half and squeeze, reserving the juice. Scrape away any white skin inside but don't damage the shells.

2 Put broken up jelly and orange juice in measuring jug, make up to 250 ml ($\frac{1}{2}$ pt) with boiling water. Stir till dissolved.

3 Stir 6 tablespoonfuls liquid jelly into cake crumbs and divide between shells. Leave shells and other jelly to set.

4 When plain jelly is firm, turn into bowl and chop. Pile into orange shells. Arrange strawberries round top of each orange.

5 Put cream in basin and whisk till thick and standing in peaks. Fit piping bag with nozzle and fill it with cream.

6 Pipe a whirl of cream on filled orange shells. Top each with 2 chocolate sticks and serve in the glasses.

Peach Melba

Ingredients
425-g (15-oz) can peach halves
3 tablespoonfuls raspberry jam
125 ml ($\frac{1}{4}$ pt) double cream
275-g (10-oz) block of vanilla dairy
   ice cream
fancy wafer biscuits

Utensils
can opener
draining spoon
plate
2 tablespoons
small sieve
2 basins
rotary whisk
fork
4 serving dishes

1 Open the can of peaches. Remove the fruit, putting it on a plate to drain. Leave the syrup in the can.

2 Put 3 tablespoonfuls jam into sieve, add 1 tablespoonful of peach syrup. Press through a sieve to make Melba sauce.

3 Place the cream in the second basin and whisk it until it is fairly stiff and thick and holds its shape.

4 Put several spoonfuls of ice cream in each of the individual dishes, piling it up attractively.

5 Place 2 of the half peaches in each glass dish, arranging them on either side of the ice cream.

6 Heap a good spoonful of Melba sauce over the ice cream and peaches. Top with the whipped cream and serve with wafers.

Fresh Fruit Salad

Ingredients
200 g ($\frac{1}{2}$ lb) grapes—green and black
  mixed
2 bananas
1 eating apple
1 tablespoonful lemon juice
2 oranges
1 pear
1 peach (if you like)
100 g (4 oz) raspberries
200 g ($\frac{1}{2}$ lb) sugar
250 ml ($\frac{1}{2}$ pt) water

Utensils
small kitchen knife
mixing bowl
chopping board
basin

tablespoon
saucepan
measuring jug
sieve
4 serving dishes

*This is just a simple fruit salad. Any type of
fruit in season can be used, such as
strawberries, cherries, apricots, mandarins.*

1 Wash grapes. Peel the green ones but not the black. Cut all grapes in half and remove pips. Place grapes in bowl.

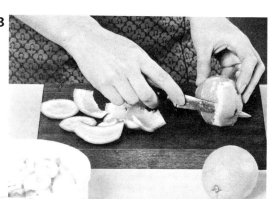

2 Peel and slice bananas. Quarter apple, remove core, slice thinly. Put fruits in basin with lemon juice, mix well.

3 Peel oranges, removing pith. Divide into segments, cutting between membranes. Add to grapes with bananas and apple.

4 Peel and quarter pear, remove core, slice thinly. Quarter and slice peach (if used). Wash raspberries, mix fruits together.

5 Put all fruit skins and pips in saucepan with sugar and water. Boil for 3–4 minutes. Cool, strain over fruit.

6 Leave syrup and fruit to get cold, then chill in refrigerator for about an hour before serving with pouring cream.

Making Tea

Ingredients
boiling water   sugar
milk   loose tea or tea bags

1 Put kettle of fresh water to boil. When it boils, pour a little into the teapot and leave the pot to warm.

2 Pour milk into jug, put sugar into basin and get teatray ready with a cloth (if you have one), cups, saucers and teaspoons.

3 Throw away the water from the pot. Put in the tea: 1 heaped teaspoonful or 1 tea-bag per person, plus "one for the pot".

4 Pour on really boiling water, three-quarters filling pot. Put on lid and leave to stand for 2 minutes before pouring.

Utensils
kettle
teapot
milk jug
sugar basin
tray
cups and saucers
teaspoons

Making Coffee

Ingredients
50 g (2 oz) ground coffee
(2 heaped tablespoonfuls)
500 ml (1 pt) water
375 ml ($\frac{3}{4}$ pt) milk
demerara or other brown sugar

1

2

3

4

1 Heat and dry measuring jug, then put the coffee into it. Warm coffee pot and milk jug with boiling water.

2 Pour 500 ml (1 pt) boiling water on to the coffee, stir thoroughly and leave to stand for about 5 minutes.

3 Heat milk in saucepan till almost boiling —but do not boil—then pour it into warmed jug.

4 Strain coffee and reheat—in the pot if it is flameproof or in a saucepan—but do not let it boil.

Some people like cold milk with coffee, so if possible serve both warm and cold milk.

Utensils

measuring jug	strainer
tablespoon	sugar bowl
coffee pot	coffee cups and
milk jug	saucers or mugs
kettle	spoons
milk pan	

Boiling Eggs

Ingredients
2 eggs   bread
boiling water   butter

1

2

3

1 Put eggs gently into boiling water. Bring water to boil again; boil 3–4 minutes.

2 Put into egg cups, cracking tops to stop hardening. Serve with bread and butter.

3 Hard-boiled eggs take 10–12 minutes. Put in cold water. Crack and remove shells.

Utensils
draining spoon   egg cups
saucepan   basin
timer   small plate

Poaching Eggs

Ingredients
butter   4 pieces of toast
4 eggs

1

2

3

1 Put water in base of poacher pan and boil. Melt knob of butter in each cup.

2 Crack eggs and pour into poacher cups. Cover and simmer for about 3 minutes.

3 Butter toast, place the eggs on it, using palette knife to ease them from cups.

Utensils
egg poacher
palette knife

Scrambling Eggs

Ingredients
butter
2 eggs
2 tablespoonfuls milk

salt and pepper
piece of toast

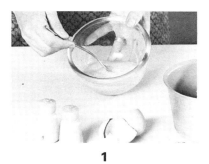

1　　　　　　　　**2**　　　　　　　　**3**

Utensils
saucepan
basin
fork

tablespoon
wooden spoon
warmed plate

1 Gently melt knob of butter in saucepan. Beat eggs with fork, add salt and pepper.

2 Add milk, pour into saucepan and cook gently, stirring as egg thickens.

3 Stir constantly till just thickened but not dry. Serve at once on buttered toast.

Frying Eggs

Ingredients
fat for frying (oil, lard, bacon fat or dripping)

eggs
bread

1　　　　　　　　**2**　　　　　　　　**3**

1 Melt some fat in frying pan but don't let it get too hot. Pour in each egg from a cup.

2 Cook gently, tilting pan so fat can be spooned over eggs (this is basting).

3 When eggs are set, lift out on to fried bread or buttered toast to serve.

Fry bread in the fat (before the eggs) until golden brown on both sides.

Utensils
frying pan
cup

cooking spoon
fish slice

warmed plates

79

Grilled Sausages, Bacon and Tomatoes

Ingredients
4 chipolata sausages, beef or pork
4 rashers of bacon
2 tomatoes
salt and pepper
pinch of sugar
butter
parsley sprigs

Utensils
kitchen scissors
grill pan and rack
fork
kitchen knife

chopping board
kitchen tongs or knife and fork
kitchen paper
serving plate

*To make this dish into a mixed grill,
cook 2 small chops and a few mushrooms
alongside sausages, bacon and tomatoes —
see pages 92–93.*

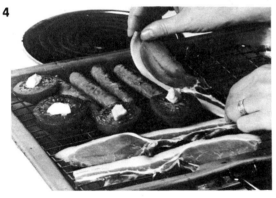

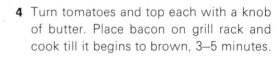

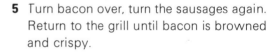

1 Light grill and leave to get hot. Cut sausages apart, place on rack and prick with fork. Grill till beginning to brown.

2 Cut rinds off the bacon with scissors. Cut tomatoes in half and sprinkle each with salt, pepper and a pinch of sugar.

3 Turn sausages over and put tomatoes alongside on the grill rack. Return to the grill for 3–5 minutes.

4 Turn tomatoes and top each with a knob of butter. Place bacon on grill rack and cook till it begins to brown, 3–5 minutes.

5 Turn bacon over, turn the sausages again. Return to the grill until bacon is browned and crispy.

6 Drain bacon and sausages on kitchen paper. Serve on a plate with the tomatoes, garnished with parsley sprigs.

Cabbage and other Vegetables

Cauliflower · Peas · Marrow · Sprouts

Ingredients

1 cabbage (or any of the other
    vegetables opposite)
salt
water
butter
sprig of mint and 1 level teaspoonful
    sugar for peas

Utensils

chopping board
kitchen knife
saucepans
skewer
colander
draining spoon
serving dishes (warmed)
teaspoon

CABBAGE

Remove outer leaves and core, shred rest finely and wash well. Bring about 2·5 cm (1 in) salted water to boil, add cabbage.

Cook cabbage (covered) about 5 minutes. Test with skewer; when tender, drain in colander. Turn into dish, dot with butter.

CAULIFLOWER

Remove outer leaves and stalk. Leave whole or cut into florets, wash well. Cook in boiling salted water 15–25 minutes.

PEAS

Shell, put into fast-boiling salted water with mint and sugar. Cook 10–20 minutes, drain, remove mint, dot with butter.

MARROW

Remove ends, cut in 5-cm (2in) rings, peel, cut in half and scoop out pips. Cook in boiling salted water 15–20 minutes.

SPROUTS

Remove outer leaves and stalk ends; cut a cross over base. Cook in boiling salted water for about 10 minutes. Drain well.

Potatoes and other Vegetables

Onions · Carrots · Turnips · Celery

Ingredients
potatoes (new or old) or any of the
    other vegetables opposite
salt
sprig of mint for new potatoes
butter
chopped parsley
milk, optional

Utensils
potato peeler
vegetable knife
bowls
saucepans
teaspoon
chopping board
serving dishes (warmed)

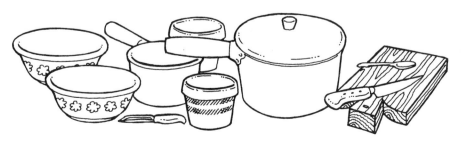

POTATOES

Peel old ones, scrape new, wash well. Put old ones in cold salted water; new ones in boiling salted water with mint.

Simmer till tender, about 20 minutes. Drain; serve with butter and parsley. Old ones can be mashed with butter and milk.

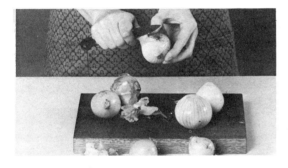

ONIONS

Peel carefully. Leave whole and boil in salted water about 45 minutes till tender; or slice or chop and fry till golden brown.

CARROTS

Peel or scrape old ones, scrape or scrub new. Cook whole or sliced in boiling salted water until tender. Serve with butter.

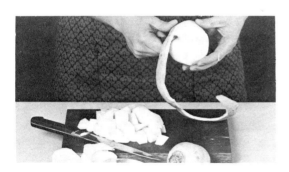

TURNIPS

Peel thickly, quarter or cube. Cook in boiling salted water for about 20 minutes. Drain, season and serve with butter.

CELERY

Trim stalks, cut in equal lengths. Wash well or scrub. Cook in boiling salted water 15–20 minutes. Serve with butter.

Roast Beef, Gravy and Roast Potatoes

Ingredients
joint of beef (topside)
salt and pepper
flour (plain or self raising)
50–75 g (2–3 oz) dripping
450 g (1 lb) potatoes
375 ml ($\frac{3}{4}$ pt) stock, vegetable water or
    (plain) water

Utensils
scales
roasting tin
palette knife
cooking spoon
potato peeler or small
    vegetable knife
saucepan
draining spoon
serving dish
basin
teaspoon
tablespoon
measuring jug
sieve
gravy boat (warmed)

See page 112 for Yorkshire Pudding to go with the Roast Beef.

1 For cooking time, allow 20 minutes per 450 g (1 lb) plus 20 minutes. Heat oven to 200°C (400°F) mark 6. Weigh joint.

2 Wipe joint and rub it with a little salt and flour. Put into the roasting tin and daub it with dripping.

3 Put the joint in the oven to cook. Baste it with its own fat once or twice during cooking. (Hold tin with a cloth.)

4 Peel potatoes and boil 5 minutes. Drain and put around meat, basting well. Allow 45–60 minutes for medium potatoes.

5 Dish up meat and potatoes and keep hot. Drain off most of the fat into a basin, leaving a little in tin for the gravy.

6 Add $\frac{1}{2}$ level teaspoonful salt, 1 level table-spoonful flour, a little pepper and stock. Stir, boil 2 minutes, strain into gravy boat.

Beef Stew

Ingredients
1 large onion
600 g (1½ lb) stewing steak
50 g (2 oz) dripping
parsley and thyme, fresh or dried
2 bayleaves
salt and pepper
40 g (1½ oz) flour
500 ml (1 pt) stock or water
225 g (½ lb) carrots

Utensils
chopping board
sharp knife
saucepan or frying pan
draining spoon
casserole
muslin and string
scissors

teaspoon
plate
measuring jug
vegetable knife
sieve
tablespoon

To turn this stew into a goulash add 2 level teaspoonsfuls paprika to the flour and seasonings and toss the meat in it before frying. Add 2 tablespoonfuls tomato paste and a 226-g (8-oz) can of peeled tomatoes to the pan with the stock. Cook as for Beef Stew, but leave out the carrots if you like.

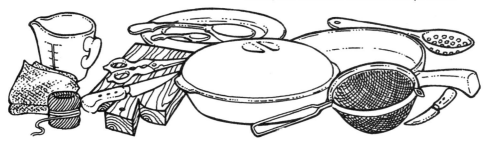

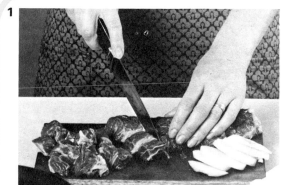

1 Peel and slice the onion. Trim meat, removing any excess fat. Cut into 2·5-cm (1-in) pieces. Melt dripping in saucepan.

2 Add onion to pan and fry till browned. Put in casserole. Tie herbs in muslin to form a bag—called a *bouquet garni*.

3 Mix 1 level teaspoonful salt and $\frac{1}{4}$ level teaspoonful pepper with the flour. Toss meat in this, then fry, stirring till brown.

4 Put meat in casserole. Add remaining flour to pan, fry gently to brown it, then add stock. Stir till thick and boiling.

5 Add *bouquet garni* and sauce to casserole, cover and bake at 180°C (350°F) mark 4 for 2 hours. Cook carrots (see page 85).

6 Remove casserole from oven and take out *bouquet garni*. Strain carrots and arrange them round the casserole.

Rice Pudding

Ingredients
butter
40 g (about 1½ oz) rice
25 g (1 oz) caster sugar
good pinch of ground nutmeg,
    optional
625 ml (about 1¼ pt) milk

1

2

3

4

1 Butter dish. Wash rice well in sieve under cold water. Drain well, put into dish with sugar and nutmeg, if used.

2 Pour on the milk, put a few knobs of butter on the top and bake in the oven at 150°C (300°F) mark 2.

3 After 30 minutes, stir pudding and return to oven. Repeat after further 30 minutes. Then cook for further 1½ hours.

4 The pudding should be creamy with a brown skin. Gently lift skin to make sure rice is done: a little milk should be left.

Utensils
pie dish (any oven
    proof dish)
sieve
measuring jug
tablespoon

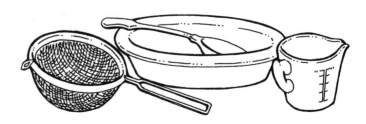

Baked Apples

Ingredients
2 large cooking apples
butter
brown sugar
25 g (1 oz) sultanas or raisins

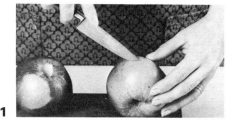

1

2

3

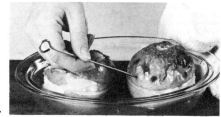

4

1 Wash apples and remove cores, using an apple corer. Cut a shallow slit through skin around middle of each apple.

2 Stand the apples in a greased ovenproof dish. Fill the holes in the middle with brown sugar and sultanas.

3 Add 2 tablespoonfuls water to dish. Put a knob of butter on each apple. Bake at 180°C (350°F) mark 4 for about 1 hour.

4 Test apples with skewer—they should be tender in the middle but not too soft. Serve as they are or with rice pudding.

Any number of apples can be cooked at the same time, provided the dish is large enough to hold them.

Some varieties of cooking apple may not take as long as an hour to cook; they should be taken out of the oven as soon as tender or the apple pulp will tend to "explode".

Utensils

apple corer	teaspoon
kitchen knife	tablespoon
chopping board	palette knife
ovenproof dish	skewer

Grilled Chops

Ingredients
2 lamb chops
salt and pepper
4 tomatoes
pinch of sugar for tomatoes
dripping or oil
100 g (4 oz) mushrooms
watercress

Utensils
chopping board
kitchen knife
grill pan and rack
small saucepan
basin
kettle
pastry brush
food tongs or knife and fork
serving dish (warmed)
fish slice

1 Pre-heat grill for 5 minutes. Trim any excess fat from chops. Season with salt and pepper and place on grill rack.

2 Cut tomatoes in half and season well. Melt fat in saucepan. Trim mushrooms and put in basin. Heat kettle of water.

3 Brush chops with melted fat and grill 5 minutes. Cover mushrooms with boiling water and leave to stand for 3–5 minutes.

4 Turn chops. Arrange tomatoes beside them. Brush both with fat and cook for 5 minutes. Drain mushrooms.

5 Put mushrooms on grill rack, brush with fat and turn chops over again. Cook for 5–7 minutes till chops are tender.

6 Arrange cooked chops, tomatoes and mushrooms on warmed dish and garnish with watercress. Serve immediately

Maxi Hot Dog

Ingredients
1 small French loaf
50 g (2 oz) butter
6–8 Frankfurter sausages
3 tablespoonfuls fruit chutney
3 slices processed cheese

Utensils
bread board
bread knife
table knife
tablespoon
palette knife
kitchen foil

Individual hot dog rolls can be used in place of French bread, allowing 1–2 Frankfurters, 1 tablespoonful chutney and 1 slice cheese per roll.

1 Put French loaf on bread board. Using bread knife, carefully cut in half lengthwise. Spread thickly with butter.

2 Arrange the Frankfurters neatly along the length of the base. Spread the chutney over the sausages.

3 Put the other half of the loaf on top of the Frankfurters. Cut a large piece of foil and wrap around the loaf.

4 Bake in the oven at 180°C (350°F) mark 4 for 25 minutes. Unwrap the baked loaf but leave it sitting in the foil.

5 Remove "lid" and cover Frankfurters with halved cheese slices. Return to oven, without lid; cook till bubbly.

6 Replace lid on loaf. Serve hot, cut into thick slices. Cooked pork or beef chipolatas can be used instead of Frankfurters.

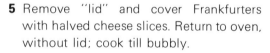

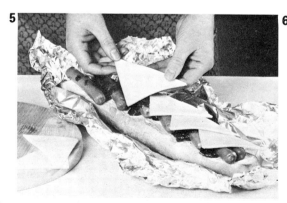

Bacon Omelette

Ingredients
2 rashers of bacon
butter
2 eggs
salt and pepper
2 tablespoonfuls water
50 g (2 oz) button mushrooms
parsley

Utensils
kitchen scissors
kitchen knife
chopping board
small saucepan
2 basins
tablespoon
fork
small frying pan or omelette pan
wooden spoon
palette knife
serving dish (warmed)

VARIATIONS
Mushroom – *Leave out bacon and chop
50 g (2 oz) mushrooms and fry and use to fill
omelette. Continue as opposite.*

Cheese – *Leave out the bacon and finely
grate 40–50 g (1½–2 oz) Cheddar cheese.
Sprinkle over cooked omelette at Stage 4
(as with bacon) and continue as opposite.*

1 Cut rind off bacon and chop rashers. Put in saucepan with knob of butter and cook gently, stirring, for 5 minutes. Keep warm.

2 Break eggs, add salt, pepper and water and beat well. Melt 25 g (1 oz) butter in frying pan; when smoking pour in eggs.

3 Cook gently till egg begins to set around edges; pull edges into centre so that liquid egg can run to side of pan and set.

4 When almost set, place the bacon in the centre. Loosen omelette around the edges with palette knife.

5 Fold a third of omelette over, turn other edge over, loosen it. Melt 25 g (1 oz) butter and fry mushrooms 2–3 minutes.

6 Turn omelette upside down on to a serving dish. Garnish with parsley and serve with fried mushrooms.

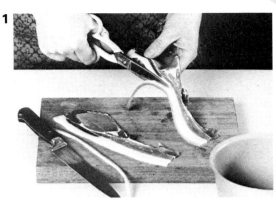

Sausage Cabin

Ingredients

450 g (1 lb) beef or pork chipolatas
1 small onion
25 g (1 oz) butter
600 g (1½ lb) potatoes
salt
50 g (2 oz) Cheddar cheese
1 egg, beaten
4 firm tomatoes
200 g (8 oz) frozen or fresh shelled peas
  (see page 83)

Utensils

roasting tin
fish slice
kitchen paper
kitchen knife
chopping board
3 saucepans
grater
potato masher

basin
fork
wooden or metal spoon
baking sheet
kitchen foil
palette knife
serving plate (warmed)
draining spoon

*Frankfurters can be used in place of the
chipolatas; and a large packet of instant
potato (4–6 servings) can be used in place
of raw potatoes.*

1 Put sausages in roasting tin. Bake in the oven at 190°C (375°F) mark 5 for about 25 minutes. Drain on kitchen paper.

2 Peel and slice onion. Melt butter in saucepan, add onion, cover and cook. Peel potatoes, cook in boiling salted water.

3 Finely grate the cheese. Drain cooked potatoes well, mash thoroughly then beat in the onion, egg and cheese.

4 Cover baking sheet with foil. Put potato mixture on it and shape into a "cabin". Halve sausages and press around sides.

5 Thinly slice tomatoes and arrange on the cabin roof to look like tiles. Use one sausage as a chimney.

6 Reheat in oven for 10 minutes. Cook peas. Lift foil on to plate, tucking it out of sight. Surround with drained peas.

Cheese and Tomato Macaroni

Ingredients
butter to grease dish
1 egg
100 g (4 oz) quick cooking macaroni
150 g (6 oz) Cheddar cheese
2 large tomatoes
1 packet parsley sauce mix, 300 ml
    ($\frac{1}{2}$ pt) size
1 packet onion sauce mix, 300 ml
    ($\frac{1}{2}$ pt) size
375 ml ($\frac{3}{4}$ pt) milk
salt, pepper and mustard, optional
few fresh breadcrumbs
sprig of parsley

Utensils
750 ml–1·1 litre (1$\frac{1}{2}$–2 pt)
    ovenproof dish
3 saucepans
egg slicer (if you have one)
chopping board
kitchen knife
grater
measuring jug
wooden spoon
skewer
colander or sieve
small basin
grill pan

*When you're told to "adjust seasoning", it
means taste the mixture you're cooking and
see if it needs any more salt, pepper and/or
mustard.*

1 Butter baking dish. Hard-boil egg for 12 minutes, shell it and cool. Slice egg lengthwise, reserving 3 slices. Chop rest.

2 Cook macaroni as directed on packet. Grate cheese. Slice tomatoes thinly, keeping 4 slices for garnish.

3 Combine sauce mixes and prepare, using 375 ml ($\frac{3}{4}$ pt) milk. Season and stir in cheese, except 1 tablespoonful, till melted.

4 Test the macaroni with a skewer. When tender, drain it and add to sauce, with all but 4 slices of tomato; mix carefully.

5 Add chopped egg and adjust seasoning. Spoon into dish; lay tomato slices on top. Mix remaining cheese and breadcrumbs.

6 Top each tomato slice with cheese and crumb mixture and brown under hot grill. Garnish with egg slices and parsley.

Poacher's Pasties

Ingredients
210-g (7½-oz) packet frozen puff
    pastry
4 streaky bacon rashers
1 small onion
225 g (½ lb) beef or pork sausage meat
    or sausages
salt and pepper
flour
1 egg

Utensils
kitchen scissors
chopping board
kitchen knife
mixing bowl
fork
baking sheet
rolling pin

saucer (14–15 cm/5½–6 in)
tablespoon
palette knife
pastry brush
basin
wire rack

*Instead of using beaten egg to glaze the
pasties, you can use the top of the milk.*

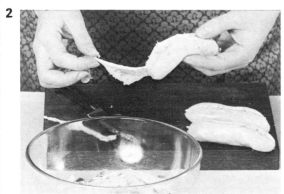

1 Leave pastry to thaw at room temperature for about an hour. Using scissors, cut off bacon rinds. Chop bacon into pieces.

2 Peel and chop onion. Remove skins from sausages if used. Mix sausage meat with bacon, onion, salt and pepper in a bowl.

3 Lightly grease baking sheet. On floured surface, roll out pastry thinly and cut into 5–6 rounds, using saucer as guide.

4 Put spoonfuls of sausage mixture into the centre of each circle. Brush edges of pastry with water.

5 Bring edges of pastry together at the top, pressing well together. Crimp between fingers and thumb. Put on baking sheet.

6 Beat egg and use to brush all over pastry. Cook at 220°C (425°F) mark 7 for about 25 minutes till golden. Serve hot or cold.

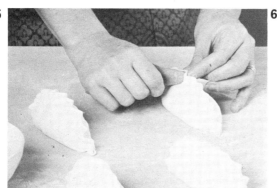

Welsh Rarebit

Ingredients
150 g (6 oz) Cheddar cheese
15 g ($\frac{1}{2}$ oz) butter or margarine
$\frac{1}{2}$ level teaspoonful dry mustard
2 level teaspoonfuls flour
2 slices bread
4 rashers streaky bacon
parsley sprigs

Utensils
grater
small saucepan
teaspoon
wooden spoon
bread knife
kitchen scissors
grill pan and rack

chopping board
kitchen knife
palette knife
fish slice
serving plate

To make Buck Rarebit, serve each Welsh Rarebit topped with a poached egg (see page 78), and with or without the bacon.

1 Grate the cheese, using the coarse side of the grater and put it into a small saucepan.

2 Add the butter and mustard. Cook over a gentle heat till cheese has melted, stirring all the time.

3 Remove saucepan from the heat and beat in the flour until it is quite smooth. Leave to cool.

4 Remove the bacon rinds. Grill with the bread till the bacon is crispy and the bread toasted.

5 Spread the cheese mixture evenly over the toast using a palette knife and making sure the toast is well covered.

6 Cook under moderate grill till golden. Serve at once topped with bacon and parsley.

Spaghetti Bolognese

Ingredients

1 onion
1 medium sized carrot
20 g ($\frac{3}{4}$ oz) dripping
350 g (12 oz) raw minced beef
1 level tablespoonful tomato paste
salt and pepper to taste
226-g (8-oz) can of peeled tomatoes
2 tablespoonfuls water
1 bayleaf
$\frac{1}{2}$ teaspoonful Worcestershire sauce
100 g (4 oz) spaghetti
grated Parmesan cheese

Utensils

vegetable knife	can opener
chopping board	teaspoon
2 saucepans	draining spoon
wooden spoon	large sieve or colander
tablespoon	2 serving plates (warmed)

To make Shepherds Pie cook meat as above and place in an ovenproof dish. Make up a packet of instant potato (2–3 servings) according to directions. Spread over mince. Cook at 200°C (400°F) mark 6 for 30–40 minutes until potato is well browned.

1 Peel the onion and carrot. Chop both into small pieces. Melt the dripping in the saucepan.

2 Fry onion and carrot for about 5 minutes, stirring occasionally to prevent sticking, until onion begins to turn pale brown.

3 Add mince and stir until thoroughly mixed. Cook for 5 minutes, stirring frequently.

4 Add tomato paste, salt, pepper, tomatoes, water, bayleaf and sauce. Boil, cover and simmer 30 minutes, stirring occasionally.

5 Boil pan of salted water, add spaghetti, bring back to boil. Cook 10–12 minutes till tender. Drain and arrange on plates.

6 Taste sauce and season again if liked. Remove bayleaf. Spoon into centre of spaghetti. Serve cheese separately.

Curried Eggs

Ingredients
100 g (4 oz) rice
salt
3 or 4 eggs
2 or 3 tomatoes
mango chutney
1 large onion
25 g (1 oz) margarine or dripping
2 level teaspoonfuls curry powder
1 level teaspoonful tomato paste
1 level tablespoonful flour
200 ml ($\frac{1}{3}$ pt) water
1 eating apple
40 g (1$\frac{1}{2}$ oz) sultanas
pepper

Utensils
3 saucepans
sieve
serving dish or plates
tablespoon
timer
chopping board

kitchen knife
2 small dishes
wooden spoon
teaspoon
measuring jug

Long grain rice, called "Patna" rice, should be used for savoury dishes, and short or round grain or pudding rice should be used for puddings.

1. Cook rice, uncovered, in boiling salted water 12–14 minutes. Drain, rinse under hot water, arrange on dish, keep warm.

2. Place eggs in saucepan, cover with water, boil for 12 minutes. Slice tomatoes and place in dish. Fill other dish with chutney.

3. Peel and chop onion. Melt fat in saucepan, add onion and fry till it begins to brown, stirring occasionally.

4. Stir in curry powder, tomato paste and flour, then add water. Bring to the boil, cover and simmer gently for 10 minutes.

5. Quarter and core apple, cut in pieces. Add to pan with sultanas, 1 tablespoonful chutney, salt and pepper. Simmer 5 minutes.

6. Peel eggs, cut in half lengthwise, place in centre of rice and spoon sauce over them. Serve with tomatoes and chutney.

Pizza Baps

Ingredients
1 small onion
25 g (1 oz) butter or margarine
1 clove garlic, optional
226-g (8-oz) can of peeled tomatoes
1 level teaspoonful tomato paste
salt and pepper
good pinch of sugar
2 bap rolls, brown or white
4 long rashers of streaky bacon
3 slices processed cheese
parsley sprigs

Utensils
kitchen knife
chopping board
saucepan
garlic crusher (if you have one)
wooden spoon
can opener
basin
fork
teaspoon
kitchen scissors
grill pan and rack
food tongs or knife and fork

1

2

3

4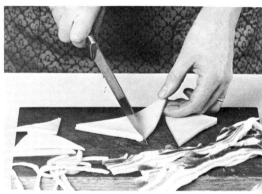

5

6

1 Peel and chop onion. Melt butter in saucepan. Peel garlic, squash with knife (or use garlic crusher), add to pan.

2 Add onion to pan and fry till soft and beginning to brown. Open tomatoes, turn into basin and break up roughly.

3 Add tomatoes, tomato paste, seasoning and sugar to pan, bring to boil. Simmer, uncovered, till thick. Stir several times.

4 Cut baps in half. Remove rinds from bacon then cut each rasher in half. Cut cheese slices into 4 triangles.

5 Place baps and bacon on grill rack. Grill baps till brown, turn and brown cut side. Grill bacon till crispy, keep warm.

6 Spoon tomato mixture on to baps, cover with 3 cheese triangles, grill till bubbling. Top with bacon and parsley. Serve hot.

Yorkshire Pudding

Ingredients

100 g (4 oz) flour,
  plain or self raising
pinch of salt
1 egg

250 ml (½ pt) milk
25 g (1 oz) lard,
  dripping or white
  fat

1

2

3

4

1 Sieve the flour and salt into the mixing bowl, then make a hollow in the centre. Break the egg into the "well".

2 Gradually work in flour, adding a little milk to give a smooth mixture. Beat well, add rest of milk, beat till smooth.

3 Put fat in tins and melt it in the oven at 220°C (425°F) mark 7 till smoking hot. Pour in batter till about two-thirds full.

4 Bake 15—25 minutes for small puddings, 25—30 for large, till risen, firm and golden. Serve with Roast Beef (see page 86).

To make toad in a hole, place 450 g (1 lb) sausages — well pricked with a fork — in a large roasting tin with 25 g (1 oz) dripping and bake for 10 minutes. Pour the batter into the tin and cook for a further 25—30 minutes until well risen and golden brown.

Utensils

sieve
mixing bowl
wooden spoon

measuring jug
palette knife
serving dish

individual Yorkshire pudding tins or
  small patty tins or baking tin about
  25·5 by 20·5 cm (10 by 8 in)

Pancakes

Ingredients
100 g (4 oz) plain flour
pinch of salt
1 egg
250 ml ($\frac{1}{2}$ pt) milk

lard or white fat
lemons
caster sugar

1

2

3

4

1 Make batter as for Yorkshire Pudding. Melt 15 g ($\frac{1}{2}$ oz) fat in frying pan. When it smokes, pour in a thin layer of batter.

2 When batter has set and is brown on one side, use palette knife to loosen and turn it over. Cook other side till browned.

3 To "toss" a pancake, slip it to edge of pan, hold handle very low down and quickly flip pancake over. No need to toss high.

4 Put pancake on plate, sprinkle with lemon juice and sugar and roll it up. Repeat until batter is used up.

Utensils
sieve
mixing bowl
measuring jug
wooden spoon
small frying pan
palette knife
fork
kitchen knife
serving plate
(warmed)

Apple Pie

Ingredients
200 g (8 oz) flour, plain or self raising
pinch of salt
50 g (2 oz) white fat
50 g (2 oz) margarine
3 tablespoonfuls cold water
600 g (1½ lb) cooking apples
50 g (2 oz) sugar
top of the milk to glaze, optional

Utensils
sieve
mixing bowl
palette knife
measuring jug
vegetable or small
  kitchen knife
chopping board

pie dish
tablespoon
rolling pin
pastry brush
baking sheet
skewer
kitchen foil

Test fruit with a skewer when the pie has been cooking for about 20 minutes and is brown. If the apples are not tender, cover the pie with foil and continue cooking for 10 minutes.

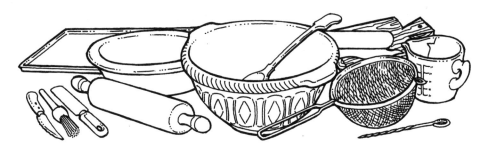

1 Sieve flour and salt into mixing bowl; rub in fats till mixture looks like breadcrumbs. Add water and bind with palette knife.

2 Peel, core and slice the apples. Arrange in layers in pie dish with the sugar. Add 3–4 tablespoonfuls water to the dish.

3 Knead pastry lightly, roll into round about 0·5 cm ($\frac{1}{4}$ in) thick. Cut off edges into narrow strips, wet dish rim and fix strips.

4 Brush pastry rim with water then carefully lift on the rest of the pastry to cover the pie. Press edges well together.

5 Trim pastry from edge of dish. Crimp edges with fingers and thumb. Roll out trimmings and cut into leaf shapes.

6 Dampen leaves, decorate pie, brush with milk. Bake on baking sheet at 220°C (425°F) mark 7 for 30–40 minutes.

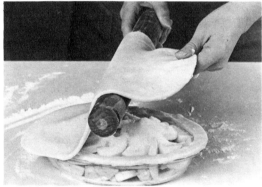

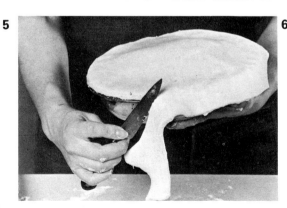

Eggomaniacs

Ingredients

4 eggs
25 g (1 oz) cheese
25 g (1 oz) soft butter or soft tub
    margarine
1 tablespoonful salad cream or
    mayonnaise
salt and pepper
2 firm tomatoes
small piece of savoury sausage or salami
lettuce or endive

Utensils

saucepan
chopping board
kitchen knife
teaspoon
basin
grater
fork
tablespoon
piping bag and plain 0·5-cm ($\frac{1}{4}$-in)
    nozzle
serving dish

**Warning — Don't eat real toadstools that look like this.
They give you terrible tummy ache!**

1 Hard-boil eggs for 12 minutes. Plunge in cold water till cold, peel. Cut small slice from pointed end of each to form base.

2 Cut another slice from the wide end to show the yolk. Scoop out yolk into a basin, using a teaspoon.

3 Grate cheese. Mash yolk thoroughly then add fat, salad cream, salt and pepper. Mix well. Fit piping bag with nozzle.

4 Stand egg whites on their bases. Fill bag with savoury yolk mixture and use most of it to fill the whites.

5 Halve tomatoes (into a top and bottom); cut 4 slices sausage 0·5 cm ($\frac{1}{4}$ in) thick. Top eggs with sausage and tomato.

6 Pipe remaining yolk mixture on to surface of tomato tops to make spots. Arrange on dish with washed lettuce or endive.

Cheese Salad

Ingredients
1 lettuce and/or endive
2 eggs
few spring onions
few radishes, optional
2 large tomatoes
$\frac{1}{4}$ cucumber
100–150 g (4–6 oz) Cheddar cheese

Utensils
chopping board	basin
salad basket or colander	fork
small saucepan	grater
kitchen knives	2 plates

Endive is a curly type of lettuce which is only available at certain times of the year.

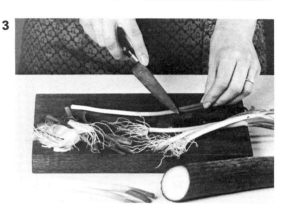

1 Remove outer leaves from lettuce or endive and wash rest in cold water. Drain in salad basket or colander.

2 Hard-boil eggs for 12 minutes. Plunge in cold water till cold, then peel. Cut into quarters or slices.

3 Cut off onion roots and trim stalks to about 7 cm (3 in). Remove radish roots and stalks (if used). Wash both well.

4 Dip tomatoes in boiling water for $\frac{1}{2}$ minute, then plunge in cold water. Hold on fork, peel off skin and slice them.

5 Wipe cucumber, then slice thinly, holding it firmly on a board. Grate the cheese, coarsely or finely—whichever you prefer.

6 Arrange ingredients attractively on plates (see picture). Serve with salad cream or French dressing (see page 122).

Tuna Stuffed Eggs

Ingredients
4 eggs
3 tablespoonfuls soured cream or thick
    mayonnaise
few chives, optional
salt and pepper
99-g (3½-oz) can of tuna fish
2 stuffed olives or 8 large capers
lettuce
1 head chicory
1–2 tomatoes
mustard and cress

Utensils
saucepan   tablespoon
timer   can opener
3 basins   piping bag and plain
chopping board   1-cm (½-in) nozzle
kitchen knife   sieve or colander
teaspoon   serving dish
fork

*If you don't have a piping bag the filling can
be spooned back into the egg whites.*

*Instead of using tuna fish, use drained
salmon or sardines if you prefer.*

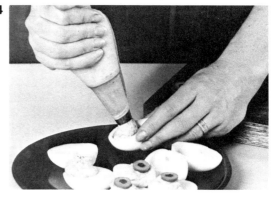

1 Hard-boil eggs for 12 minutes, plunge in cold water and leave till cold. Remove shells and cut eggs in half lengthwise.

2 Scoop out egg yolks carefully into basin and mash with fork. Add soured cream, chopped chives (if used), salt and pepper.

3 Open can of tuna fish and drain off the oil. Mash thoroughly then add to the egg mixture and beat until very smooth.

4 Fit piping bag with nozzle and fill with tuna mixture. Pipe into each egg half. Top with piece of olive or a caper.

5 Wash lettuce and chicory and drain thoroughly. Arrange on dish. Cut tomatoes in wedges. Wash mustard and cress.

6 Place stuffed eggs on the salad and garnish with tomatoes and mustard and cress. Serve with crusty bread and butter.

Salade Niçoise

Ingredients

2 eggs
lettuce leaves
1 large boiled potato
4-cm (1½-in) piece of cucumber
few chives or spring onions
99-g (3½-oz) can of tuna fish
2 tomatoes
4 stuffed olives, optional
French Dressing
4 tablespoonfuls oil
1 tablespoonful vinegar
1 tablespoonful lemon juice
salt and pepper
¼ level teaspoonful sugar
¼ level teaspoonful French mustard

Utensils

saucepan   kitchen scissors
timer   can opener
2 basins   fork
sieve or colander small jug
salad bowl   tablespoon
chopping board   teaspoon
knife

Well drained anchovy fillets and cooked French beans can also be added to this salad.

1 Hard-boil the eggs 12 minutes, plunge in cold water till cold. Wash and drain lettuce. Tear into pieces, arrange in bowl.

2 Cut potato in small cubes and dice the cucumber. Put into a basin. Snip chives, with scissors, into basin.

3 Open tuna fish and drain off the oil. Break the fish into small pieces and add to the potato mixture.

4 Cut each tomato into 6 slices. Slice olives (if used). Remove shells from eggs and cut each egg into quarters.

5 To make dressing, put ingredients in jug and whisk with fork till blended. Pour over tuna mixture and "toss" till mixed.

6 Spoon tuna mixture over lettuce, garnish with tomatoes, olives and eggs. Serve with French bread and butter.

Coleslaw Salad

Ingredients
225 g ($\frac{1}{2}$ lb) white cabbage
2 sticks celery
1 large carrot
1 eating apple
$\frac{1}{2}$ lemon
3 tablespoonfuls soured cream or
   natural yogurt
3 tablespoonfuls thick mayonnaise

salt and pepper
25 g (1 oz) shelled walnuts
40 g (1$\frac{1}{2}$ oz) sultanas
50–75 g (2–3 oz) sliced garlic
   sausage or other sausage
50 g (2 oz) sliced liver sausage
parsley sprigs

Utensils
chopping board
kitchen knife
grater
mixing bowl
2 basins
lemon squeezer
large tablespoon
fork
serving dish

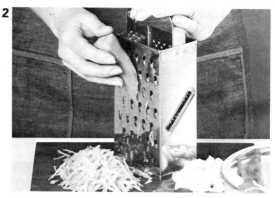

1 Remove core from cabbage and then shred (see page 18). Cut the celery into thin slices.

2 Peel carrot then grate on the coarse side of the grater. Place in bowl with the cabbage and celery.

3 Quarter apple, remove core, chop into small pieces and put in basin. Squeeze lemon, add juice to apple, mixing well.

4 Mix soured cream and mayonnaise together in a basin. Add salt and pepper to taste then mix in apple and lemon juice.

5 Chop walnuts, add to cabbage with sultanas and apple mixture. Toss together till well mixed and coated in dressing.

6 Spoon coleslaw on to serving dish and arrange garlic and liver sausage around the edge. Garnish with parsley sprigs.

Index